Stuck in the Dark

maria castro

BookLeaf
Publishing

India | USA | UK

Presentation by *BookLeaf Publishing*

Web: www.bookleafpub.com

E-mail: info@bookleafpub.com

ISBN: 9789357215367

First edition 2022

*Dedicated to Arthur, George, Ernie, Barbie,
Flakiss, Percy, Coco, and all my dogs past,
present, and future.*

Not imaginary

You randomly messaged me
We video chatted right away
Decided to keep in touch

Talked to you for two years
Almost every day, no pause
Met in person as many times as pigs fly

Flew halfway around the world
Just to meet you in person
Felt like a higher plane of existence

Even if we do not last
You opened my eyes
The world is not as dark

As that one side of the moon

Sticking your fat head out the wrong window

Feet pounding while trying to hide
Looking for the source of the bullets
Being wary of campers

Hear a noise from outside the house
Edge closer to the nearest window
Prepare M16 to fire

BOOM!
Fall back and watch the brief replay
Wasn't quick enough to spot the culprit
Revive and continue losing like always

Drink your happiness

I twist open the cap
And start sipping like there's no tomorrow
Feel the bubbles slither down my throat
The sweet taste confusing me
How is it possible for it to be zero calories?
I graze on this for a few more hours
Like I'm a cow out on the pasture
Don't know why I do this every time
Finally, I throw out the empty bottle
My second Diet Coke today
Have to stop, I'm like a bottomless pit for it
Never satisfied in the end, mouth always open
Need another substitute, still searching for it
Like if it is Atlantis or Bigfoot

How it used to be

Turning on the old PlayStation 2
Inserting the Drakan game disc
Fighting through the monsters
In Surdana, in Ravenshold, in Kragmor
Filling up the magic, melee, and archery trees

Switching to Metropolismania later
Marking roads with the magic chalk
Moving in fussy people to the skeleton town
Harassing them to get new people to move in
Lather, rinse and repeat until stage goal is met

Get bored with such games and other books
Look at side to see Ernest, licking his paws
Barbie and Flakiss, chilling on the sofa
And out the window to observe
Arthur, George and Percy playing in the
backyard

Mess with the three Chihuahuas close to me
Offer them little milk bones after playtime
Go outside to get Percy to chase me
Also give Arthur and George plenty of rubs
Throw pieces of chicken their way

Finally go online to favorite site
To get the daily chance reward
Scroll through the dumbest forums
Read the most ridiculous threads
Dress my avatar the way I would if I was thin

Less than a man

Attracting like magnets
With small talk here and there
Flowing easily, like water down a drain
First meeting was magical
Next meeting planned immediately
Going the same way
That's why it was surprising
How easy it was for everything else to come
Not just first but only
The magic died down easily
Like helium inhaled into the lungs
Better to be brutally honest
And say the magic was just an illusion
From the beginning

Go away

We're alone together
Chatting and joking around
The warmth wrapping us together
Then you just press your lips on mine
Go away

I try to keep the peace
Very stupid of me
I let your tongue barrel towards my throat
Trying to let this wash over me, like a cold
shower
Go away

Later, we are out on the town
You lead me around, mansplaining traffic to me
I laugh it off, trying to focus on the plan
You hug me forcefully when we return to the
room
Go away

Seriously
Just go away

Go away
Go away
Go away

Laughing at the office

Pull in the parking lot
Almost nudge the next car
Step out and go inside
The nearly empty building
Grab a tea and watch videos
Everyone either at home
Or on some break
So the day is slow
Walk around barefoot
Watch more videos
Skits of teachers
Parody songs
Clips of old SpongeBob
Twenty four
Something funnier
Twenty five
Cackle some more
Keep scrolling
Finally, it's almost dark
Gather up the torture devices
And walk on out
If only wasting time felt
As good as it does
At the office

Loud adult

I used to just go for it
Say what was on my mind
Make the stupidest jokes
Not caring about who disagreed
Or who spoke up

Then as I aged
I started to watch myself
As if I was a toddler
Who couldn't stop searching
For ways to off myself

I lay awake sometimes
Wondering what happened
That made me go from a loud kid
To a boring, quiet grown up
At least I'm outspoken inside

Never satisfied

Look for a new song
Find one with a memorable beat
Runs through my head
Like a dog fleeing a bath
Repeat it as if it were
Something to study for
Then get bored of it and hit shuffle
And keep going back
To the old, tired songs
That sent me to the new one

Home

Left to find independence
But kept flying back to the nest
On and off for multiple years
Until just before graduation
Hibernated there until
A new opportunity shone
Over the horizon
Flew over there
On a one way ticket
But the new ray of sunshine
Was short-lived
Winter daylight basically
Went back home yet again
Until a new lucky break
And dwelling opened up
Now wondering
If there will ever be
A place that is all my own
Where I will be happy
For many years to come
The word eludes me now

Fireworks

It must feel good
It must feel really good

To annoy others for no reason
Not even waiting for a holiday
To be super loud and over the top
To scare others who were not expecting it

Especially dogs and other furbabies
Extra if they are missing or lost
Trying to make their way back home
Feeling like it is the end of the world already

It must feel good
It must feel really good

To have no such things in mind
To not care for others
Not see beyond myself
Be easily impressed by some loud jangly keys

It must feel good
It must feel really good

Autopilot

13

Waking up and making a to do list only to throw away the entire day on the laptop. Twisting the quote that said that time one enjoyed wasting wasn't wasted just to make myself feel better. I wrap myself with this as if it were a shawl.

Just an excuse

14

I see interesting books, knick knacks, skincare, endless items online. I buy and forget about them once I put them away. I say I have to finish what I already have before using the new ones. I never do, only to throw them all away, regift them, or donate them. Almost always, I pass them to others. Why can't I stop? Why can't I just stick to what I have? Why am I trying to fill my life with things to avoid being by myself?

For the thrill

Both of them have nothing to do
Bored with the typical school day
And a home life made up
Of cute but messy dogs
Video games and internet surfing

They decide to ditch school one day
Walk to the nearby McDonald's
To have a meal they saved up for
Before heading to the nearby drugstore
To use the five finger discount on makeup

Feeling the rush
Awake in their typical existence
They continue with this
Until they realize they are sloppy
And don't want to risk their futures

The makeup never made its debut
Mostly used for swatching
And at home joke looks
But it did not matter
The temporary escape was enough

Idiot

Trying to build a mansion
One fit for a socialite
With enough space to entertain
A boatload of acquaintances
Fit an open bar
An area for a live band
Several banquet tables
And a dance floor

Place the walls for an entrance
And some others for the halls
Continue with the rest
Until the hours go by
And it is too late for dinner
Not enough time for the socialite
Get frustrated the next day
And give up on the house

After some time
I kick myself in my thoughts
For not using the prebuilt homes
On any Sims custom content site
Cannot believe I did that
Cannot believe I wasted my time
Focusing on the minor details
Instead of the story

Regret

17

Should have stood up and stuck with an old friend instead of trying to focus on what I thought was important - fleeting "popularity" in elementary school that affects your life as much as a hangnail.

Choices

You're supposed to declutter your items to make
your move easier
At least that's what most people tell me
It's just hard to decide what you will or won't
need soon or later
Especially when you lie to yourself everyday

Monotonous breaks

Sleep all freaking day
Play the same games
Watch the same channels
Read the same sites
Over and over again
All day

Make excuses
For not being active
For not focusing on others sometimes
For not being productive on goals
Over and over again
All day